The Kids' Business Book

by Arlene Erlbach

Lerner Publications Company
Minneapolis

*For Ms. Lesley Williams, who knows the business
of being a librarian*

This book would not have been possible without
the generous help of the following people and organizations:
Ms. Nancy White and Ms. Jackie Geschickter at
National Geographic World magazine.

The publisher would like to thank Jenna Browning, Jessica Donovan, Kelly
Donovan, Beth Jacobson, Sonia Jacobson, Cody Reisner, Chris Simondet, Jeff
Sweetser, and Downie Winkler who were photographed for this book.

Series Editor: Martha Brennecke
Series Designer: Zachary Marell
Photographers: Jim Simondet and Nancy Smedstad
Electronic Prepress: Mike Kohn and Jane Conway

Copyright © 1998 by Arlene Erlbach

This book is available in two editions:
Library binding by Lerner Publications Company, a division of Lerner Publishing Group
Soft cover by First Avenue Editions, an imprint of Lerner Publishing Group
241 First Avenue North
Minneapolis, MN 55401 U.S.A.

Website address: www.lernerbooks.com

Library of Congress Cataloging-in-Publication Data
Erlbach, Arlene.
   The kids' business book / by Arlene Erlbach.
     p.   cm.
   Includes index.
   Summary: Profiles business owners who began their businesses
between the ages of seven and twelve, describes simple methods of
starting a business, and includes tips on accounting and advertising.
   ISBN 0-8225-2413-9 (lib. bdg. : alk. paper)
   ISBN 0-8225-9821-3 (pbk. : alk. paper)
   1. Small business—Management—Juvenile literature. 2. New business
enterprises—Management—Juvenile literature. 3. Money-making projects for
children—Juvenile literature. 4. Entrepreneurship—Juvenile literature. [1.
Moneymaking projects. 2. Business enterprises.
3. Entrepreneurship.] I. Title.
HD62.7.E75   1998
658.02'2—dc20   96-34131

Manufactured in the United States of America
5 6 7 8 9 10 – JR – 08 07 06 05 04 03

The Kids'
Business
Book

CUSTOMERS

INVENTORY

BUSINESS PLAN

SUPPLIERS

PUBLICITY

CONTENTS

Kids Are Business People, Too

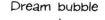

Dream bubble

Have you ever dreamed of having lots of money? Have you ever wanted to have enough cash to buy video games and clothes, without begging your parents? Even if you're too young to get a job, you can still make money for yourself. You can start your own business.

Every year, thousands of kids go into business for themselves. They earn extra money beyond their allowance, to spend or to save. Some kids have used their business earnings to pay for trips, lessons, or save for college. And these kids don't all baby-sit or mow people's lawns. Many kids have formed unusual businesses, or found ways to make their businesses different and special.

Kids who own businesses are entrepreneurs. Entrepreneurs are people who start and manage any type of business.

Entrepreneurs are good planners and organizers. Before they start their businesses, they find a need and think about how to fill it. They decide if their businesses should be similar to existing businesses or not. Maybe they will form a business like others, but they'll offer something extra or charge less than their competitors. Some entrepreneurs start entirely new and different kinds of businesses.

Having a business isn't always easy, but it's usually challenging and fun. And of course, it earns money for you. First let's meet some kid entrepreneurs. Then you can learn about how to start a business of your own.

Meet Kids in Business

Owner:
Scott Klocksin
Started Business:
Age 11

Scott's Lemonade Stand

8

Scott at work

Scott went into business because he needed a bike. He didn't lock his bike when he went to the pool, and it was stolen. His parents told him, "If you want another bike, you'll have to pay for it yourself."

Scott didn't have enough money for a bicycle. Since he doesn't get the kind of allowance that would let him save for a bike, Scott decided to go into business. "I

thought that selling food might be a good idea," he says. "Since it was summer, I decided to try a lemonade stand."

Scott borrowed $12 from his mother to buy frozen lemonade concentrate. He set up the stand in front of his house. Scott lives on a busy street that's near a jogging and bicycle path, so he thought he'd get lots of business. People get thirsty after exercising in the hot sun. But not as many people stopped for lemonade as Scott had hoped.

Scott thought about what he could do to attract more customers. He decided to move his stand where more people would see it. He set up his stand right at the bicycle path.

Relocation did the trick. Scott sold all his lemonade in less than an hour. So Scott called his parents on a portable phone they'd lent him in case he had any problems. He needed more lemonade fast!

The next weekend, the local grocery store ran out of lemonade concentrate. Scott's dad bought a case of cans of prepared lemonade instead. The cans sold even better than the lemonade made from concentrate. It was easy to keep the canned lemonade cold in an ice chest. And people didn't worry about its cleanliness.

Scott buys his cans of lemonade by the case of 48 cans, at a warehouse store, for about $10. So Scott's lemonade costs him about 20¢ a can. He sells the cans for 75¢. Scott makes 55¢ on each lemonade sale.

The first month, Scott made over $100. He's sure he'll have $260 to buy the bike he wants before the summer ends. But he plans to stay in business. "I'll probably have my lemonade stand again next summer," Scott says. "I like the food business a lot. When I grow up, I'd like to own a coffee shop."

Owner:
Meggie Ennis
Started Business:
Age 10

Meggie's Dog-Walking Service

"I love dogs and other animals," says Meggie. "I have three animals of my own: my dog, Woodley, and two rats, named Ying and Yang."

Having her own pets made Meggie aware of a fact: Lots of people love their animals, but they don't always have the time or energy to take care of them. Dogs are especially difficult to care for, because they need walking. So Meggie asked some neighbors if they'd like Gilda, their Golden Retriever, walked when they were too busy or at work. Gilda's owners liked Meggie's idea a lot. For three walks and one feeding, Gilda's owners paid Meggie $7. Meggie started taking care of Gilda whenever Gilda's owners needed to work late or were out of town.

Meggie and a client

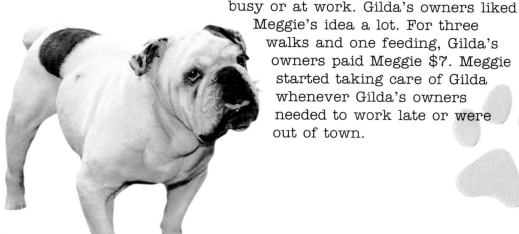

A few other neighbors saw Meggie with Gilda, and they asked Meggie about walking their dogs. Meggie gained two more regular canine customers, Spanky and Tonya.

Each dog needs slightly different treatment. Tonya doesn't always need to go for a walk. Her owner just pays Meggie to let her out, play with

Meggie's got a head for the animal business.

her, and clean up after her. "That's the yucky part of the job," Meggie says. "But I have to do that with all the dogs I walk, anyway."

Spanky is more work than Tonya or Gilda. Spanky wears a sweater and knit booties during her winter walks. Spanky doesn't like wearing her knitted outfit, so she squirms when Meggie dresses her. And Spanky likes her food cut into tiny pieces. Still, Meggie thinks the extra work for Spanky is worth it. Seven dollars a day to walk, dress, and feed a dog is good money for a 12 year old.

Besides these dogs, Meggie looks after a hamster when its owners are out of town. Meggie would definitely like to expand her business and deal with all types of pets. She wants to be a veterinarian when she grows up. Meggie also likes earning money for doing something that she considers fun.

Owner:
Jason Fullone

Started Business:
Age 8

Jason

Jason's Birthday Party Store

Jason knows exactly what both kids and adults enjoy a lot: birthdays and balloons. When Jason was eight years old, he began selling balloons at the indoor flea market where his mom sold music boxes. Jason charged $5 for each balloon. After he paid for balloons and his helium tank rental, Jason made about $60 every weekend!

In New York state, where Jason lives, child labor laws are very strict. Jason couldn't legally be involved in a business where it might seem like he was working for his mom. So Jason applied for his own business license under the name DBA Jason Balloons. DBA means "doing business as." This would prove that Jason worked for himself—not for his mom. "I'm the youngest person in my county to register a DBA," Jason says.

When Jason's mom decided to move her business to a regular shop, Jason tried a new business inside her store. He wanted to expand his balloon business to something more. At The Birthday Party Store, Jason sold everything for

birthdays—wrapping paper, gifts, candles, and personalized tapes that play "Happy Birthday to You."
He even sold stuffed animals that play "Happy Birthday" when somebody pulls their tails.

Jason worked at his store every weekday from 3:00 to 6:00 p.m., and all day on Saturdays. He made about $200 each month. That gave him plenty of money to save and spend. "I liked being at my store more than hanging out," Jason says. "It was interesting and fun. I did homework when no customers were around."

About a year later, Jason's mother got another job and closed her business. Jason didn't have a place to keep his business anymore, so he went out of business.

"I probably wouldn't have as much time for the store, now," Jason admits. "School takes up more time, since I'm in junior high, and I've become more involved in sports."

Yet The Birthday Party Store was such a unique and popular idea that people still remember it. They're disappointed that it's out of business. "I miss the store, too." Jason says, "I'd like to own a party store again, when I grow up."

Who are these masked phantoms? Jason and his mom.

Owner:
Alison Brill
Started Business:
Age 8

Alison's Baby-Sitting Service

Alison describes herself as very responsible, organized, and flexible. These traits are very important for any baby-sitter.

Alison and the triplets: Ben, Alex, and Nicky

"Ever since I was five years old I've been responsible," Alison says. "My mom bought me a hamster and a fish when I was five, and I took good care of them."

One of Alison's neighbors heard about how responsible she is. The neighbor needed help when she was pregnant with triplets. She hired Alison to weed her garden and help her around the house. She was impressed with Alison's work, so she trusted Alison to help her after the triplets were born.

At first Alison helped feed, burp, and hold the three baby boys. She also learned to carry the triplets around and play with them. She sorted laundry or helped around the house. Eventually Alison baby-sat for the triplets when their parents went out.

How to feed 11 kids: 1. Take a slice of bread... 2. Spread with peanut butter...

The job with the triplets developed into more business. Soon Alison had so many people calling her that she sometimes referred customers to a friend. And ever since the triplets have grown into toddlers and are more active, Alison has had a friend help her sit with the boys. Alison and her friend are each paid $2.50 an hour. That's less than Alison would make if she sat for the boys by herself. But Alison says she'd rather make less money than take on a difficult situation alone.

Once some of the neighborhood moms wanted to go out for lunch, and they hired Alison to sit for their kids—11 kids all together! Alison asked her friend to help her this time, too. They made peanut butter sandwiches for lunch and took the kids to the park. The girls each made $15 that day.

Alison is willing to sit for kids other sitters may be hesitant to watch. Soon she'll be sitting for twin toddlers and a boy with Down Syndrome. "All kids have some type of problem that baby-sitters have to deal with," Alison says. "Sometimes it just doesn't seem so obvious."

Alison's flexibility and responsibility have made her a very popular sitter. During the summer, Alison's business brings in $20 to $50 a week. She's used her earnings to buy new video games, and she's saved quite a bit of money, too. She plans to take some of the money she's earned to overnight camp for spending at the camp's trading post. And she'll do more sitting after she returns.

3. Add jelly... 4. Fold or slice, then serve...

5. Repeat 10 times.

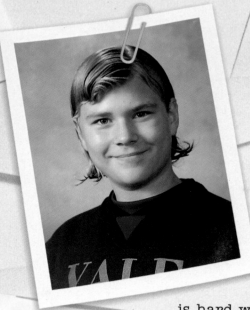

Owner:
David Kahl, Jr.
Started Business:
Age 11

David's Better Letters

David Kahl knows that for many people, writing letters is hard work. Besides having to think of what to say and writing your letters, you need to gather addresses, stamps, stationery, and pens. Often these things aren't in just one place, so it takes a while to get everything together. That's why David invented and sells "Better Letters."

Better Letters is a kit for writing letters. It includes a folder with pockets that hold letter-writing materials, and a 65-page book. The book shows examples of many kinds of letters people need to write. The book also contains addresses that people can use to write away for sports cards.

"I borrowed $1,000 from my parents to start my business," David admits. "And I conducted a survey to make sure people would really buy Better Letters."

To survey his potential customers, David typed up and copied a questionnaire, which asked if people would buy Better Letters, what the kit should contain, and how much they'd pay for it. He passed out the copies to local businesses and to people at the post office. Every one of the 40 people David questioned liked his idea, so David decided to make and sell the letter-writing kit.

The complete Better Letters kit: everything you need

One of the problems with making the kit was finding a folder with all the pockets it needed—10 in all. David couldn't find this kind of folder, so he had the folders for his kit specially made. He learned that the more folders he had made at once, the less each kit would cost.

Better Letters kits cost David about $9 each. He sells them for $13.95, so he earns about $5 per sale. Local stationery and novelty shops carry David's product. David's dad and mom help sell his product, too. David's dad is an educational consultant and school principal, and David's mom teaches high school English. They've sold Better Letters to teachers, who use the book to show students how to write letters.

How does David spend the money he earns? "I spend some on myself," David says. "Some I save for college." David also sponsors a local Little League team.

Owner:
Colleen Flynn
Started Business:
Age 10

Colleen's Bead Jewelry

"My business started out as a fad two years ago," Colleen says. "Lots of girls were making bead jewelry. I decided to design jewelry, too. I realized that making jewelry was more than a fad for me. It was a way that I could express myself."

Colleen spent more and more time on her bead creations. She designed earrings and bracelets to match most of her outfits. Colleen's mom liked a bracelet Colleen had made from silvery, star-shaped beads. She offered to buy it for $5.

Colleen felt she could sell her jewelry to people besides her mom, and she thought about going into business.

A few weeks later, a neighbor put out flyers announcing a garage sale. Colleen knew this would bring people to her neighborhood. The day of the garage sale, she set up a card table in front of her

house and displayed her bead earrings and bracelets. Her sale was a success. In a few hours, Colleen made over $20.

Colleen began to hold jewelry sales in front of her house every few weeks. And when Colleen's neighborhood held a craft fair, she set up her business there. In one day of the fair, Colleen made over $100.

At the craft fair, a woman asked for a bracelet in red, white, and green—the colors of the Italian flag. The woman was of Italian descent. This gave Colleen an idea. She could offer to make jewelry in the colors of other flags, too. In Chicago, where Colleen lives, people are from many different cultures. Colleen is half Irish and half Colombian, and she is very proud of her heritage. She understands how people enjoy wearing jewelry that suggests where they or their ancestors came from.

Now Colleen offers many kinds of custom jewelry. She makes earrings and bracelets in any color scheme that her customers want. She can assemble the pieces in about 15 minutes.

Colleen plans to exhibit and sell her jewelry at more art fairs. "The money is good in bead jewelry," she says, "and designing custom jewelry gives me the chance to help other people express themselves."

Your place for custom beadwork: Colleen's traveling jewelry stand

Owner:
Matt Inukai
Started Business:
Age 8

Matt's Magic Act

Matt's got something up his sleeve...

Matt's business started with a gift from his mom when he was eight years old—a magic kit. "I was super interested in that magic kit," Matt says. "As soon as I got it, I started to do tricks."

"I first performed for my sister, Ellie, and brother, Danny, who were four and six at the time. They were impressed, and so was my mom. She told our neighbors about me, and I gave them free performances." Soon people began hiring Matt.

By the time Matt was nine years old, he scheduled a show almost every weekend. He charged about $15 for each show. By the time Matt was 11, he earned $50 per show. Now he charges $75. This is less than the $90 to $150 adult magicians in his area charge.

"Except for the initial magic kit, I bought all of

my illusions with my own money," Matt says. Illusions are the equipment and supplies needed for the tricks magicians perform.

"The reason I've been so successful is that I can really relate to kids, since I am one," Matt explains. "My customers tell me that I'm just as good as an adult. Some families have hired me year after year."

Matt also does benefit shows at hospitals and retirement homes. He performs free, each year, for the Juvenile Diabetes Association. He also did a show for no charge at his sister's school.

This year, Matt will put an ad in the Yellow Pages for the first time and go to his first magician's convention.

Matt's advice to would-be magicians: Make up an act, practice, and do shows at first for free or very little. Eventually people will recommend you.

Owner:
Brandi Champion
Started Business:
Age 10

Brandi's Dolls

Brandi is true to her last name—Champion. She's an honor student, and Brandi is the owner of her own handmade doll company, Brandi's Dolls.

"I've always liked working with my hands," Brandi says. "After my grandmother took me to a doll-making class, I wanted to make a doll at home."

Brandi made the doll's body from a string mop. She made the head from cotton balls covered with fabric. Then she painted a face and gave the doll a wig and accessories.

"I planned to give the doll to my teacher," she says. "But someone offered to buy it for $25."

Brandi knew she had a product people would buy, so she began making more dolls. She sells them at art shows and craft fairs, where she has so far always been the youngest exhibitor. She also receives special orders from people who have heard about her work.

Each of Brandi's dolls is an original. A doll sells for $25 to $60, depending on the accessories the doll wears. Brandi dresses some of her dolls with necklaces, bracelets, earrings, and barrettes. She even designs dolls carrying tiny bouquets of silk flowers. The grandmother who took Brandi to the doll-making class is a floral designer.

Brandi's Dolls

Each night after Brandi finishes her homework, she works on a doll. In addition to school and dollmaking, Brandi volunteers at a senior citizens' center. She may even teach a class on dollmaking at the senior citizens' home.

Where does all the money from the dolls go? Brandi says, "Almost every cent goes right into my college fund." Brandi plans to be a doctor, lawyer, or a buyer for a department store.

Jessica & Krista's Sports Card Design

Owners:
Jessica Mendelowitz & Krista Lowe
Started Business:
Ages 12 & 12

Jessica (left) & Krista (right)

Photograph by Bob Wellinski

Jessica and Krista love baseball and baseball cards.

"When I was in sixth grade," Jessica explains, "I saw a notice on the LaPorte Middle School bulletin board about doing an extra school project. I knew exactly what I wanted to do—something related to baseball cards, and something that would be a business."

Jessica discussed the idea with Mrs. Wiley, her special projects teacher. They came up with a business idea that would involve baseball cards and the baseball team at the local high school. They decided to make baseball cards just like ones that are sold for major league players, except that their cards would feature the high school's players.

This was a big project. It involved gathering detailed information about each player and getting a photograph of each

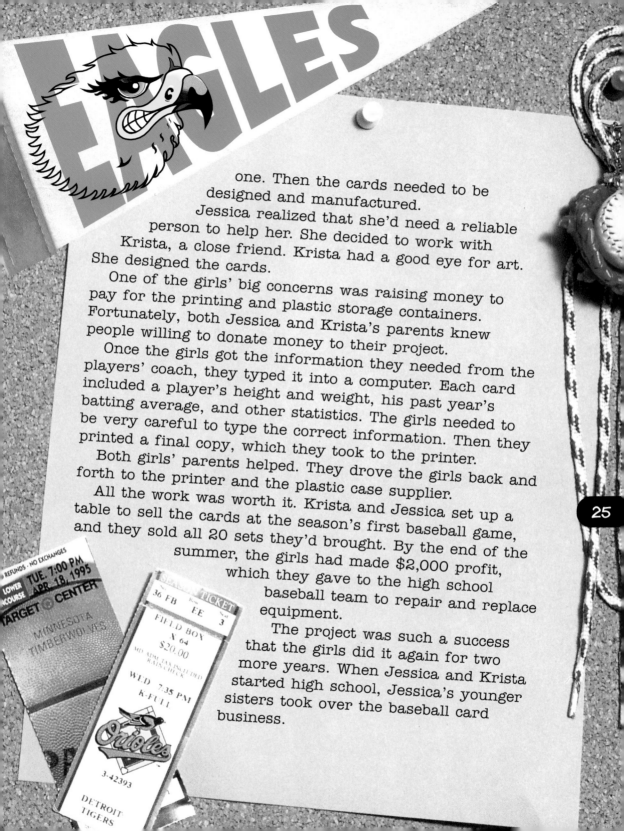

one. Then the cards needed to be designed and manufactured.

Jessica realized that she'd need a reliable person to help her. She decided to work with Krista, a close friend. Krista had a good eye for art. She designed the cards.

One of the girls' big concerns was raising money to pay for the printing and plastic storage containers. Fortunately, both Jessica and Krista's parents knew people willing to donate money to their project.

Once the girls got the information they needed from the players' coach, they typed it into a computer. Each card included a player's height and weight, his past year's batting average, and other statistics. The girls needed to be very careful to type the correct information. Then they printed a final copy, which they took to the printer.

Both girls' parents helped. They drove the girls back and forth to the printer and the plastic case supplier.

All the work was worth it. Krista and Jessica set up a table to sell the cards at the season's first baseball game, and they sold all 20 sets they'd brought. By the end of the summer, the girls had made $2,000 profit, which they gave to the high school baseball team to repair and replace equipment.

The project was such a success that the girls did it again for two more years. When Jessica and Krista started high school, Jessica's younger sisters took over the baseball card business.

Jake digs rocks.

Owner:
Jake Jabusch
Started Business:
Age 7

Jake's Garnet Mining

Few kids would even think about mining and selling garnets for a business, but that's exactly how Jake Jabusch earns over $1,000 each summer. He collects and sells a special type of garnet found near his home in Wrangell, Alaska. Tourists who visit Wrangell each summer buy the garnets. A few days a week, Jake waits for the tourist ferries to dock. Then he shows the tourists his garnets, which he displays in a plastic tray.

Tourists pay from 25¢ to $50 for each garnet, depending on its size and quality. A scratched garnet earns much less than one in good condition. People buy the garnets and have jewelers set them into rings, earrings, or pendants. Other people like pieces of rock with garnets inside. They use the rocks for paperweights, bookends, or just for decoration.

Jake's garnet sales are busiest from June until September, when Alaska tourism is heavy. But in the spring months, there's plenty of preparation involved. First Jake and his family mine the garnets at a spot called the Garnet Ledge. The garnets must be collected without power tools, according to the wishes of the person who willed the Garnet Ledge to the children of Wrangell and the Boy Scouts of America. It takes at least a day's work of chiseling, by hand, to gather a good supply of garnets.

Jake has plenty of competitors in the garnet business. About 10 other kids meet the ferries, too. But Jake has always been one of the most successful garnet sellers, because he's always polite to customers. He doesn't lose patience answering the same questions again and again, like "What do people do for a living here?" and "What's it like to live in Alaska?"

Jake's older brother, Mike, used to sell garnets, too. That's how Jake became involved in the business.

Jake gives people business cards, and some people have ordered garnets through the mail. Jake makes about $1,500 a year on the mail-order business, which he splits with his brother and mom. Jake's mom does the mailings. Jake even has one customer in Copenhagen, Denmark.

Jake only works on the garnet business every other day during the summer. The other days, Jake admits, "I veg out, go swimming, or relax in the city park's hot tub."

Jake digs boats, too. (with Cody)

Owner:
Kira Kufersburger
Started Business:
Age 8

Kira's Gingerbread Houses

Many kids dream about gingerbread houses at Christmastime. Kira does, too, and she expertly decorates them. Every weekend, from November to Christmas, Kira frosts gingerbread houses and puts candy on them. She does her job so well that some people don't feel right about eating her houses.

Kira's family owns a bakery in Green Forest, Arkansas. That's how Kira became involved with the gingerbread houses. When Kira was eight years old, she was at the bakery watching her mom make gingerbread houses for the holiday season. This fascinated Kira, who was just tall enough to reach the table. She wanted to help, so her mom let her decorate a house she'd just assembled. Kira did such a great job that she's decorated houses for the bakery ever since.

First Kira's mom assembles each house, which is made from sheets of gingerbread dough. Then Kira takes over. It takes Kira about 20 minutes to decorate each house. For her work, she earns about $3.50 an hour. Each Christmas holiday season, Kira earns about $300.

Kira helps decorate gingerbread people, too. Her family's bakery makes special gingerbread people with flowers on them, to sell when the University of Arkansas has its football games.

After a while, Kira gets sick of gingerbread houses and people. So she's usually glad when the football and Christmas seasons end.

In addition to making gingerbread houses, Kira paints rocks so that they look like animals—cats, rabbits, and scarabs. She sells the stones for $5 to $10, depending on the size of the stone.

"The stones are something I do when I'm in the mood," Kira says. "They aren't really a business, but they do bring in extra money once in a while."

Rocks are Kira's hobby.

Owner:
Mike Pearson
Started Business:
Age 12

Mike's Teaching T-shirts

"My business sprung up by accident," Mike Pearson explains. "I love social studies and learning about my roots," he says. "So when my grandmother visited Africa, her photographs and stories about the trip fascinated me."

Mike's interest in his grandmother's trip inspired him to paint a map of Africa on a T-shirt with puffy paints, just for fun. Mike's family and friends liked his creation so much that he hired a printer to silk screen his design on 100 shirts. He gave them away as gifts.

Mike learned that his T-shirt appealed to more people than his family and close friends. He had other people asking to buy the shirts from him.

Soon Mike started selling the shirts for $10 apiece. He calls the shirts "Teaching T-shirts," because the map helps people learn about Africa. Wearing a Teaching T-shirt is like wearing a geography lesson. The map shows all the African countries with names and boundaries, plus the continent's major rivers.

Mike sells the shirts to teachers' supply stores. "Social studies teachers like to buy the shirts when

Mike's a student
and a teacher.

they teach classes on Africa," Mike says, "and people enjoy wearing them." Sometimes Mike receives special orders from groups or individuals who have heard about the shirts.

Recently, Mike was the T-shirt coordinator for a Jack and Jill International Convention. Jack and Jill is a community service organization for African-American youth. Mike was in charge of making sure that 3,000 T-shirts were printed.

Mike makes about $2,000 each year from his Teaching T-shirts. All of the money goes into his savings for college.

To Mike, school comes first. "I don't get too involved in my business when it has any chance of interfering with schoolwork. That's the most important thing for any kid to be involved in."

Starting a Business

Going into business means making lots of decisions and having a business plan. Successful entrepreneurs take time to plan their business before they start. They ask themselves many questions. You can answer questions about your business in a business journal or notebook.

Start by thinking about your business goals. Do you want a short term business that earns money for a specific item, like a new bike, musical instrument, or pet? Do you want an ongoing business that brings in steady money? Or

Good planners get ideas here...

maybe you'd like to only run your business during school vacations.

You'll also need to think about how much time you'll be able to spend on your business. Be realistic. If you already are expected to do lots of chores at home, you won't have as much time to devote to your business as a kid who has few family obligations. Ditto if you take lots of lessons or have the hardest teacher at school this year.

What Do I Like and What Am I Good At?

Most important, your business should be something you think is fun and something that's easy for you to do. To help you decide what kind of business to try, make a chart like the one below. Write down what you like to do and what you're good at. Then jot down businesses related to your likes and talents.

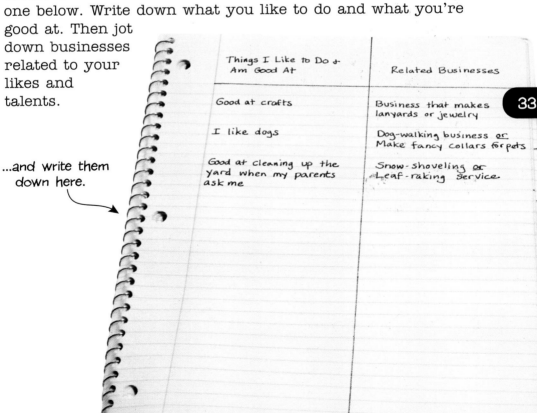

...and write them down here.

Things I Like to Do & Am Good At	Related Businesses
Good at crafts	Business that makes lanyards or jewelry
I like dogs	Dog-walking business or Make fancy collars for pets
Good at cleaning up the yard when my parents ask me	Snow-shoveling or Leaf-raking Service

Your manufacturing business could be making lanyards (also known as friendship bracelets).

Some businesses are service businesses. Others are manufacturing businesses. Service businesses provide care, maintenance, or repair to customers—such as dog walking, yard cleaning, or lawn mowing. Customers pay service businesses to do things they themselves don't have the time or desire to do. Most kids have service businesses, because they cost less to run than manufacturing businesses, and they are easier to start.

Manufacturing businesses make and sell products, such as jewelry, dog collars, or lanyards.

Manufacturing businesses usually cost more than service businesses, and they require

This service business has gone to the dogs.

more preparation, but they can be very profitable as well as creative. Manufacturing businesses are especially good for artistic people.

What Is the Business Market?

Would enough customers need what your business offers? This is something very important to think about before you start.

Let's look back at your list. A snow shoveling business sounds great—if you live where it snows a lot, and if there are houses around you. But if you live in a neighborhood of condominiums or apartments, you might not get much business. The management for these buildings has probably made other arrangements for snow removal.

Is there another service you could offer in your community? In a neighborhood with lots of apartment buildings and condominiums, there may be a lot of older people. Maybe some of these people would like you to pick up their groceries, newspapers, or dry cleaning for them when the weather is cold and snowy. They may even need your services in good weather.

When you ask yourself these questions, you are analyzing the business market for an area. You are thinking about the people in that area, finding a need they have, and filling that need. Keeping your market in mind is a great start for brainstorming business ideas. Just follow these steps:

1 Think about items or services that might be needed in your neighborhood.

2 Think of a business that already exists in the area. Could you perform the same service, or provide a similar product, better or at a lower price?

3 Ask your family, neighbors, and friends what business they think is needed.

4 Make a list of the results, then ask yourself if the businesses are activities you would enjoy and be good at doing.

Businesses Needed in My Neighborhood	Would I Like to Do It?
Dog clean up	No!
Delivery service	Yes— but I'll need to buy a wagon.
Birthday party helper	Yes – I love birthday parties. Won't need to buy a wagon.

What do you like to do? Be honest!

Can You Run the Business Yourself?

A lot of businesses are small operations that you could manage by yourself. But some businesses work out better if you run them with another kid, or if you ask an adult to sometimes help you.

Maybe you've decided on a birthday party business. This business may sound okay to do alone. But if you live in a neighborhood where most birthday parties include an entire kindergarten or first-grade class, you'd be better off doing this with a friend. You would have to split your earnings with your friend. But even though you would make less at each party, you would probably do such a super job that customers would recommend you to others.

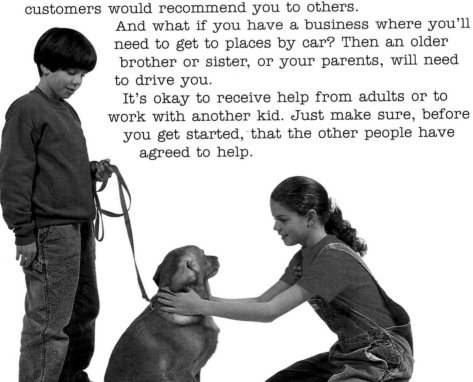

And what if you have a business where you'll need to get to places by car? Then an older brother or sister, or your parents, will need to drive you.

It's okay to receive help from adults or to work with another kid. Just make sure, before you get started, that the other people have agreed to help.

What's in a Name?

Make sure you give your business a name that tells people what your business does and attracts customers. Lots of businesses use straightforward names that tell who's in charge of the business and what it does—names like "Bud's Weeding Service" or "Tonya's Dog-Walking Service." Or you might like to use a catchy name that people will remember, such as "Teaching T-Shirts," "Weed It Out," or "Walk Your Dog."

Don't use the initials *Inc.* or *Corp.* after your business name unless you've incorporated your business. When a business is incorporated, it means that papers have been

filed with the state, and the state recognizes the group of people who run the business as a single person. Adults in business do this to simplify their taxes and to avoid being sued if the business has big problems. It's illegal to say your business is incorporated if it's not.

You also shouldn't copy the name of somebody else's business. It belongs to them, and they can legally stop you from using it. You may want to have an adult check out business names in your state to see if the one you want is already being used. You can register your own business name with your state to make sure nobody else uses it.

Look in a business directory for ideas, but don't copy a name.

four

Money, Profit, and Taxes

The reason anyone goes into business is to make money, of course. But it usually takes at least a little money to start a business. That's a reality all entrepreneurs face.

Start-Up Costs

Tools of the trade cost money.

The money you need to begin a business are the business's start-up costs. Your start-up costs may be small, or you may need to invest in a lot of equipment. Before going into business, list all the materials your business might need. Let's say you're starting a business where you'll do gardening. The first items on your list will be a spade, a weeder, and gardening gloves. You might also find customers who will want you to spread fertilizer or weed killer, and they'll expect you to supply it. You'll need a wagon for carrying your equipment and supplies from house to house. So your list of expenses might look like this:

BUD'S WEEDING SERVICE

Equipment & Supplies: Start-up	Cost
Advertising: 100 flyers at .05 apiece	5.00
Trowel	5.00
Spade	5.00
Weeder	5.00
Gardening gloves	5.00
Weed killer & sprayer	7.00
Wagon (have, but need to paint) — paint,	10.00
Total costs	42.00

Now you'll need to think about how to come up with your start-up costs. For most kids' businesses, start-up costs come from savings, loans from parents, or money raised. Maybe you can raise money for your business by doing extra chores for your parents, or by selling old toys and games. Raising your own start-up costs will make you look like a serious entrepreneur.

Pricing

People usually hire kids to do a job for three reasons: They like to help kids, they think kids are cute, and they like to save money. Adults know they won't be expected to pay a kid the same price they would pay an adult. Adults usually need the money they earn to pay living expenses and support a family. You can charge less. Your money is going to pay for life's fun and extra stuff.

Whatever adults' reasons are for hiring kids, you must charge enough for your goods and services to make money. You also need to keep your prices low enough to attract customers. How do you find the right price? It can be tricky to do, and for a while you may have to try different prices, to see what works.

The best way to figure a fair price is by checking out the competition. Look at businesses similar to yours that are run by adults and by kids. If you charge only a half or a third of what an adult would charge to do the same job, you'll gain customers. If your competition is other kids, set your price a little lower than theirs. If kids with experience shoveling snow charge $10 to do a job, offer to do the same size job for $8. As you become more experienced, you can raise your price.

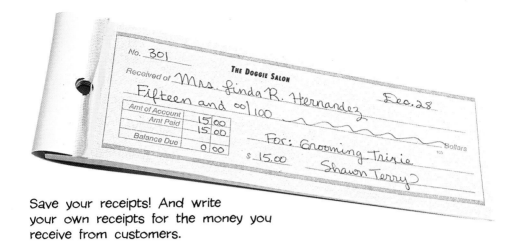

Save your receipts! And write your own receipts for the money you receive from customers.

Income - Expenses = Profit

Three very important words in business are income, expenses, and profit.

Income is the money you take in from a business.

Expenses are the money it costs to run your business, like what you spend for supplies and equipment.

Profit is what you have left after you subtract your expenses from the income.

Whenever you perform a service or sell merchandise, list the amount you collected in your business notebook or journal. Put this on a page titled "Income."

Whenever you buy something for your business, you'll receive a slip of paper called a receipt. Save it. This is proof of money spent. Keep your receipts in an envelope inside your business journal. Label this envelope "Expenses."

You should figure your profit weekly, and make sure your business is making money. If you are losing money, you will need to adjust your prices or reduce expenses.

To help you track your income, expenses, and profit, make a chart like the one on the next page. To make sure everything is correct, have an adult check your business worksheet for you.

Tonya's Dog-walking Service
month of August

	Income	Expenses		Profit
Week 1	Bobo – 4.00 Spotsy – 6.00 Jocko – 4.00 Lulu – 10.00 24.00	Dog biscuits, 1 box – 5.00 Plastic bags – 1.00 6.00	24.00 – 6.00 =	18.00
Week 2	Bobo – 6.00 Jocko – 8.00 Lulu – 7.00 21.00 (Spotsy moved)	Flyers to attract new customers to take Spotsy's place – 5.00	21.00 – 5.00 =	16.00
Week 3	Bobo – 6.00 Jocko – 7.00 Lulu – 6.00 19.00	None	19.00 – 0 =	19.00
Week 4	Bobo – 6.00 Jocko – 6.00 Lulu – 9.00 King – 15.00 36.00	Jeans – 20.00 (ripped when King pulled me so hard I tripped)	36.00 – 20.00 =	16.00
Total for August	100.00	31.00	100.00 – 31.00 =	69.00

Figure your business income,
expenses, and profits in a notebook...

Other Expenses: Advertising and Taxes

44

Your start-up costs are not the only expenses you'll have in running a business. You will have to keep buying supplies when they run out. And you may want to set aside some money for other costs, such as advertising and taxes.

Advertising means spreading the word about your business. It can cost a little or a lot, depending on how creative you are. There are many options for advertising that are discussed in chapter 5.

PUBLICITY

INVENTORY

CUSTOMERS

BUSINESS
PLAN

...or on a computer.
Back up your files!

Taxes are something you've probably heard your parents discuss. Taxes are the money that workers and businesses pay to the government to keep it running. Each state and city government has its own laws about taxes and how they are paid. A parent can check this out for you, or you can ask about local taxes at a public library.

In addition, the United States government has regulations that apply to all U.S. citizens. If you make $400 or more in one year, you must file forms with the Internal Revenue Service. You'll also pay tax on the money you made. This is called self-employment tax. You may be subjected to income tax, too. The rules on income taxes change often, so have a parent or another adult check with a tax advisor.

It is important that an adult help you fill out any tax forms. If they're incorrect, the forms will be sent back and you might be fined. You won't be excused just because you're a kid.

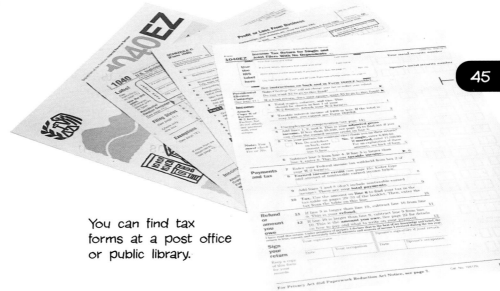

You can find tax forms at a post office or public library.

Savings Accounts

The money you make from
your business needs to be
stored somewhere. Small
amounts—$25 or less—can
be kept in a strong metal box
with a lock. It's good to have a
small amount of money around for regular expenses and
making change. But you should keep larger amounts of
money in a bank.

Keeping your money in a bank can earn you more money,
because the bank will pay you to keep money there. This
payment is called interest. Let's say you have $100 in a
savings account, paying 6 percent interest per year. In one
year, you'll make $6. That's not much. But if your business
does well and you have $1,000 in the bank, you'll make $60
in a year, just by keeping your money in the savings account.
Not bad, considering you didn't need to lift a finger to earn it.

You can set up your account as a personal account—under
your own name—or as a business account, under your
business name. Every bank has its own rules about opening
accounts for kids. When you open your account, you'll
probably need an adult to go with you.

Checking Accounts

If you have a business where lots of expenses need to be
paid, you may need a checking account. You've probably seen
your parents write checks. A check is a promise to pay
somebody. That somebody must "cash" the check to get the
money—they must take the check to the bank, in order to

receive the amount of money written on the check. They can either receive it in cash, or the amount will be paid directly into that person's bank account.

At the end of each month, your bank will send you a statement of your account. The statement will list the deposits you made in the month, the checks that were cashed against your account that month, and your account balance (the amount of money left in the account).

Along with your statement, you may receive the actual checks you made out to people that they cashed. These checks, called canceled checks, are stamped on the back. They are "canceled" because their value—the money they were worth—was paid out on them, and the amount of each check was subtracted from your checking account balance. Be sure to keep canceled checks. They can be used as receipts to track business expenses.

Remember what you bought with each check. Write yourself a note on the memo line, such as "supplies," or "business expenses."

Passing the Word

Every business needs advertising. Otherwise, nobody will know that your business exists. Flyers, business cards, newspaper ads, and premiums are all inexpensive ways to advertise your business.

Flyers

One of the most inexpensive and effective ways to advertise is with flyers. They are ads printed on sheets of paper that you can hand out to people, mail, or post on bulletin boards. Depending on how many copies you print, flyers may cost from 3¢ to 10¢ or more for each copy. To check prices, look in your Yellow Pages under copy shops or printers.

TUFF TURF
LEAF & LA
SERV
WEEDING·M
EDGING·R
FERTILIZ
NO JOB TOO SMALL/NO D
LOW RATES·R
CALL FOR A QUOTE ON Y
LEAF + LAWN SSS-7164
LEAF + LAWN SSS-7164
LEAF + LAWN SSS-7164
LEAF + LAWN SSS-7164
LEAF + LAWN SSS-7164
LEAF + LAWN SSS-7164

Flyers need to be neat. They should include at least these things:

1. Your name and your business name

2. Your phone number or address

3. Information about what services or products your business offers

4. Your prices (optional)

To create a flyer, you can draw or write by hand on a white, 8½ x 11-inch piece of paper. Many kids use a computer desktop publishing program to create flyers. You'll need just one original flyer, then you can take it to a copy shop or printer to have it reproduced. Be sure to keep the original, so you'll have it when you need to get your flyer reprinted. A good place to keep the original is in your business journal.

Think carefully about the places you want to pass out your flyers. Take them where people who would likely use your service or products will see them. For example, post flyers for a dog-walking service at a pet shop or a veterinarian's office. Hang flyers for a lawn-mowing or weeding service at a gardening shop. Hand out flyers to individual homes, too. If you know the people who live in a particular neighborhood, think about whether or not they could use your goods or services.

This flyer has handy tear-off tabs.

Flower Power

SEEDLINGS FOR YOUR GARDEN
&
POTTED PLANTS
555-6878 / ask for Jade

Your card says something about your personality, and your business style.

Leo's Cat Sitting

Call for appointments: 555-1112

The Write Type

We type anything
Color printing
Files on disk

Danny - 555-4249 / Ellen - 555-6146

Business Cards

Business cards are actually small versions of flyers. They usually cost from $15 to $25 for 500 or more. Give business cards to customers who have inquired about your business from the flyer. Offer extra business cards to customers who would like to recommend you. Business cards make you look professional.

Newspaper Advertising

Every newspaper has a special part toward the back called the classified advertising section. The newspaper charges advertisers much less to advertise in the classified section than in the main part of the paper. Potential customers scan classifieds when they need something very specific, like a clown or magician for a party, or a lawn-mowing service. In some towns, newspapers offer a special classified section and discount for advertising kids' businesses.

Newspapers charge classified advertisers by the word or line. So you'll need to be very careful about wording your ad. Your ad needs to contain enough information to attract potential customers, of course. But don't include unnecessary information that customers can find out once they call you.

Here are some examples of classified ads and how to figure what they would cost:

Seventeen words at 50¢ a word will cost $8.50. Telephone numbers are often counted as two words.

Four lines at $5 per line will cost $20.

Twenty-four words at 75¢ each will cost $18.00.

Ad-Only Papers

Many communities have "ad-only" newspapers. These newspapers carry little or no news, and mostly ads. Their rates are low, because they have a small readership. They are passed out free to homes, or people can pick them up in stores or restaurants. Ad-only papers are the perfect place to advertise your business. People often read these newspapers looking for the goods and services that small businesses offer.

Advertise in your community or neighborhood. The rates will be lower, and your customers will live nearby. Unless you live in a small town, it's not necessary to advertise in a city's major newspaper.

Clipping coupons cuts costs for customers.

Premiums

Do your parents use coupons? Have you ever received a free sample? Offers that are free or priced less than normal are called premiums. They encourage potential customers and create interest in a product or service.

You may want to offer a coupon for a dollar or more off your regular price. If you're a performer, such as a magician or clown, do some free shows to attract customers. If you make jewelry or T-shirts, give friends a few free samples to wear.

Jake Jabusch made the news.

Free Publicity

Sometimes you can let people know about your business without paid advertising. That's right—because you're a kid who's in business, you may be very interesting to a community newspaper.

Community newspapers always need articles about local citizens. Once you've been in business a while, have one of your parents call the newspaper and tell them about your business. Maybe a reporter will come to your house and interview you. A photographer may even take your picture.

In some communities, newspapers have special children's sections that focus on information about local kids. Check them out—or maybe your school paper would like to do an article about you and your business.

A potential customer looks over Jake Jabusch's wares at the city's dock.

10-year-old earns up to $120 an hour

(Photos by Kim Bradford)

By KIM BRADFORD

As Jake Jabusch sets up shop on the city dock in front of Wrangell, passengers off the cruise ship Dawn Princess walk by, casting a wary eye to his plastic tray of purple-red stones perched atop an old rusty TV tray.

One middle-aged woman ... moment and Jak...
a-half ...

Jake raises his face and squints ...
crystal blue eyes lay hid ...
lashes. He re ...
"Yes," ...
lookin ...

53

Mayor's legacy shines on for young garnet peddlers

By SUE CROSS
ASSOCIATED PRESS

Wrangell, Alaska — A mayor's gift of a mountainside of garnets to the children of this remote island town has turned two generations of its youngsters into industrious gem dealers.

Paper routes and lawn mowing provide small change compared to the $1,000 or so that a Wrangell child can earn each summer by hawking garnets to cruise ship passengers and other tourists.

Crowds of children meet almost every ship at the Wrangell waterfront, carrying their gems in everything from muffin tins to Tupperware. Some stand shyly and depend on tourists' curiosity to draw customers, but most warble, "Wanna buy a garnet?"

Tourists pay anywhere from a quarter for a pea-sized purple gem to $20 or more for a golf ball-size garnet embedded in a chunk of the silvery schist from which it was chiseled.

The garnets come from a mountainside at the mouth of the Stikine River, on the mainland about nine miles from Wrangell.

The property was willed to the Boy Scouts of America in 1962 by Fred Hanford, a former mayor of Wrangell, a town of about 2,100 in southeastern Alaska. Under the terms of the gift, only Boy Scouts and the children of Wrangell have may mine an... ...nets.

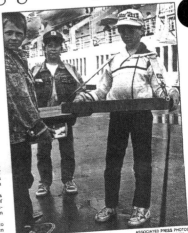

ASSOCIATED PRESS PHOTOS

Young garnet peddlers (above, left to right) Mike Jabusch, 11, Bob Sorrel, 10, and Toby Dow, 11, wait for cruise ship's tourists to disembark at the Wrangell, Alaska, dock. Jake Jabusch, 7 (right), is among the youngest and most successful at selling the industrial-quality stones.

Staying in Business or Going Out?

All businesses go through changes or have problems that good entrepreneurs must take care of. These changes or problems usually happen because:

1 Your business grows so fast that no kid (or even an adult) could handle all the business.

2 Your business isn't making enough profit or attracting enough customers.

3 You have raised enough money or have just grown tired of your business, and you want to close it.

Too Much Business

Maybe you've started a business hoping to make a few dollars on weekends and after school. It seems like things are really booming. New customers constantly call and demand your products or services. But you don't really have the time to take care of everyone. This can be a great position to be in, but it's kind of scary.

Maybe your business is a dog-walking service and you'd only planned on three or four regular pooches to walk. But lots of people have seen you with your four-legged clients and have started calling you.

The first thing you might think about is walking two or three dogs at a time. But it's probably not a good idea to walk two dogs from different households at once. They may not get along. Then you'll have more trouble than the extra money is worth. You could take on more dogs, separately. But if you did, this may start to interfere with homework or the time you spend with your friends. No matter how devoted someone is to a business, he or she usually has other interests and responsibilities.

There are a number of ways to solve the problem in a professional way. These methods can be applied to a number of businesses.

Business can be busy...

...or slow.

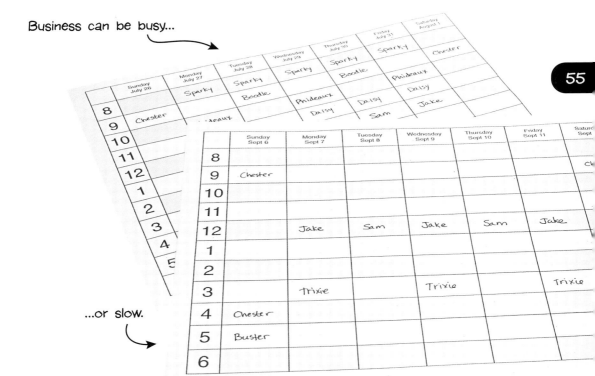

One solution is to tell certain customers, "I'm sorry, I'm booked for now." Tell the customers you'll call back when your schedule isn't so tight. Maybe you could refer them to another kid in a similar business.

Another solution is to ask a friend or sibling if they'd like to work with you. You can still make money off the deal, because you can take a small portion of the money they make. For example, if your helper makes $3 for every dog he or she walks, you could ask your helper for 50¢. You earned the money fairly, if you were responsible for getting the customer. But if your helpers find customers on their own, it's only fair to let them keep their full earnings. You should also allow them to charge whatever price they want.

If a business grows too fast, it's usually best to turn down business or arrange for help. The worst thing you can do for your business is take on more than you can handle and not do the job well. Then you'll start losing business.

When Things Aren't Going Well

Sometimes you may need to change your business plans in order to make your business more successful. When things aren't going well, think about what's causing the problem.

Is your price high enough to make a profit? Make sure you aren't paying too much for materials and supplies. Or is your price too high? Check out the competition again. Your price may need to be lower to attract new customers.

Is there too much competition for your products or services? If there is, you can add extra services to your business, or revise your product to make it extra special.

Another way of dealing with competition is to expand your business into another neighborhood.

Is there enough demand for the products or services you sell? Maybe your business is seasonal, so you don't attract enough customers to make a good year-round profit. You might need to go into a different type of business.

Other kids decide they want to go out of business entirely. Perhaps you've grown tired of your business, no longer have time for it, or you've raised the money you needed to save. Maybe you just don't like the business as much as you thought you would. There are lots of reasons that people go out of business, and there is no need to feel bad about doing it. Politely tell your customers that you're going out of business. You don't need to give them a reason. If another kid has a business similar to yours, refer your customers to that person. Or you may want to hand your business over to a brother, sister, or friend.

Final Paperwork

After you've closed your business, you should prepare a final business statement to show if you've had a profit or loss. You may need to file papers with your state or federal government and close your business bank account. It is important to discuss the closing of your business with an adult. A wise entrepreneur ends a business in the same organized fashion he or she started it.

Becoming an entrepreneur is challenging and fun. Besides earning extra money, running a business helps you develop new skills—some that you may never have known you had. Good luck on starting your business, and may it be a success!

More Information

For More Reading

Barkin, Carol and Elizabeth James. *Jobs for Kids.* New York: Lothrop, Lee & Shepard, 1990.

Berg, Adriane G. and Arthur Berg Bochner. *The Totally Awesome Business Book for Kids.* New York: Newmarket Press, 1995.

Berg, Adriane G. and Arthur Berg Bochner. *The Totally Awesome Money Book for Kids* (And Their Parents). New York: Newmarket Press, 1995.

Burford, Betty. *Chocolate by Hershey: A Story about Milton Hershey.* Minneapolis: Carolrhoda, 1994.

Gold, Rebecca. *Steve Wozniak: A Wizard Called Woz.* Minneapolis: Lerner, 1994.

Madama, John. *Desktop Publishing: The Art of Communication.* Minneapolis: Lerner, 1993.

Otfinoski, Steve. *The Kids' Guide to Money.* New York: Scholastic, 1996.

Pile, Robert B. *Women Business Leaders.* Minneapolis: Oliver Press, 1995.

Scott, Elaine. *The Banking Book.* New York: Frederick Warne, 1981.

Weidt, Maryann N. *Mr. Blue Jeans: A Story about Levi Strauss.* Minneapolis: Carolrhoda, 1990.

Wilkinson, Elizabeth. *Making Cents: Every Kid's Guide to Money.* Boston: Little, Brown, 1989.

Other Resources

Lots of organizations exist to help kids in business. Some publish newsletters. Others offer business camps, or they will send people out to schools to teach kids all about business. Here are a few of these organizations.

Business Kids
One Alhambra Plaza, Suite 1400
Coral Gables, FL 33134
For $9.95 you can join Business Kids and receive their quarterly newsletter. The newsletter has interesting stories about kids and their businesses and useful ideas and tips. You'll also receive a kit and a special hot line number to find out more about problems unique to kids in business.

Homeland Publications
2615 Calder
League City, TX 77573
This software publisher makes a program that helps you design business cards and forms.

Junior Achievement
National Headquarters
One Education Way
Colorado Springs, CO 80906
(719) 540-8000
http://www.ja.org
Junior Achievement has offices in many major cities, and it will set up programs at schools all over the country. The organization offers business education programs for grades K–6, 7–9, and 10–12.

National Federation of Independent Businesses
Education Foundation Awards Program
Attn: Kate English
53 Century Boulevard, Suite 300
Nashville, TN 37214
phone: (615) 872-5384
fax: (615) 391-5874
e-mail: kate.english@nfib.org
Each year the NFIB awards a prize of $1,000 to someone who has created and managed a successful business by age 21 or younger.

National 4-H Council
7100 Connecticut
Chevy Chase, MD 20815
301-961-2800
Ask for pamphlet called "Let's Start a 4-H Business."

Zillions
P.O. Box 54861
Boulder, CO 80322-4861
This magazine for kids is from the publishers of Consumer Reports. Zillions *contains regular features on earning and spending money.*

Glossary

balance: the money left in a bank account when deposits have been added and cashed checks have been subtracted

classified ad: paid advertisement placed in a special section of the newspaper

competitor: someone who tries to get the same customers you do

DBA: abbreviation for "doing business as"

entrepreneur: person who starts and manages a business

expense: what it costs to run a business. The money a business pays out.

income: the money a business takes in

premiums: offers that are free or priced less than normal to encourage customer participation

profit: the money that is left over when expenses have been subtracted from income

publicity: advertising to let people know that your business exists

receipt: written proof of money spent

Index

About the Author

Arlene Erlbach has written more than 30 books of fiction and nonfiction for young people. Her book *Video Games* was a 1996 selection for the ALA's list of Quick Picks for Young Adults, a list of books recommended for reluctant young readers.

In addition to being an author, Ms. Erlbach is an elementary school teacher. She loves to encourage children to read and write, and she is in charge of her school's Young Authors' program. Ms. Erlbach lives in Morton Grove, Illinois, with her husband, her son, a collie, and two cats.

Acknowledgments
The photographs on the following pages are reproduced with the permission of: page 10 (top), Ministry of Forests/Forestry Canada; page 10 (bottom), Thomas P. Benincas, Jr.; page 11 (bottom), Colleen Sexton; page 24 (girls), Bob Wellinski; pages 26-27 (Sitka coastline), Visuals Unlimited, © Ernest Manewal; page 26 (garnet), Visuals Unlimited, © Arthur R. Hill. Artwork on page 25 (pennant), page 31, and page 50 by Chad Herges.